D0386617

An Ali Cat Christmas

story by Dandi Daley Mackall

pictures by Janet McDonnell

Katy loved Christmas.

She loved Christmas trees.

She loved to wrap gifts.

But most of all, Katy loved to open
her gifts on Christmas morning.
And tomorrow was Christmas.

Katy shook a small box.

"Here's one for you, Ali Cat."

Ali Cat ran and hid behind Mom.

"Ee-yew!" said Ali Cat.

"I don't think Ali Cat loves
this part of Christmas,"
said Katy's mother.

TO:
KATY

"Why do we have to go to Granny's

on Christmas Eve?" asked Katy.

"I don't want to leave my gifts."

"We'll be home in time
to open gifts tomorrow morning,"
Mom said.

"Hear that, Ali Cat?" Katy asked.

But Ali Cat looked happy
to go to Granny's.

"I've missed you!" Granny said.

Katy hugged her granny and said,

"I missed you too!"

Granny smelled good, like cookies.

"Meow," said Ali Cat.

"Merry Christmas to you too,

Ali Cat," Granny said.

"Granny's tree is so little,"

Katy told Ali Cat.

"And there are only three gifts."

Katy shook her gift.

"It's socks," she told Ali Cat.

"Granny always makes us socks."

"Katy, look!" Granny called.

Katy ran to the window.

"It's snowing!" Katy shouted.

Snow fell fast and hard.

"Looks like we may get

a white Christmas," Mom said.

Soon, the snow was deep.

"Come on, Ali Cat!" Katy said.

Katy and Ali Cat dashed outside.

Ali Cat licked the snow.

Katy made snow angels.

Mom and Granny came outside.

"Let's make a snowman!"

Mom said.

"I have a better idea,"

said Granny.

They rolled balls of snow.

Granny made snow ears.

"Use donuts for eyes," Granny said.

"It's a snow cat!" Katy shouted.

Inside, Ali Cat purred by the fire.

Katy thought about her gifts at home
under her big tree.

"Is it time to go?" Katy asked.

Mom looked at Granny.

"There's too much snow," Mom said.

"Katy, we can't drive home tonight."

"What about Christmas?" Katy said.

Granny kissed Katy's cheek and said,

"It will be Christmas here too."

"No it won't," thought Katy.

"Not without our gifts."

Granny made a bed by the tiny tree

for Katy and Ali Cat.

Mom, Granny, and Katy read the story

of the first Christmas.

"Mary and Joseph weren't home

for Christmas," Katy said.

"I'll bet they slept on the floor,

like me."

Katy woke up to a wet nose.

Ali Cat was licking her.

"I wish we had our gifts,"

Katy told Ali Cat.

Ali Cat just purred.

"Merry Christmas!" said Mom.

Mom and Granny kissed Katy.

Katy opened her gift from Granny.

"Thanks for the socks," she said.

"Merry Christmas," Granny said.

"Merry Christmas," Katy said back.

And it did feel like Christmas.

"Look! The snow stopped," Mom said.

"I guess we can go home now."

But Katy saw how happy Ali was.

And so was Granny.

And so was Katy,

even without all her gifts.

"Mom?" Katy asked.

"Could we stay here longer?

Ali Cat and I are having

a very merry Christmas!"